Glendale Library, Arts & Culture Dept.

2.6

CHILDREN'S ROOM

NO LONGER PROPERTY OF
GLENDALE LIBRARY,
ARTS & CULTURE DEPT.

Zoom In on Rocks and Minerals

Rocks

Andrea Rivera

j 552 RIV

abdopublishing.com

Published by Abdo Zoom™, PO Box 398166, Minneapolis, Minnesota 55439. Copyright © 2018 by Abdo Consulting Group, Inc. International copyrights reserved in all countries. No part of this book may be reproduced in any form without written permission from the publisher. Abdo Zoom™ is a trademark and logo of Abdo Consulting Group, Inc.

Printed in the United States of America, North Mankato, Minnesota
032017
092017

THIS BOOK CONTAINS RECYCLED MATERIALS

Cover Photo: Koji Hirano/Shutterstock Images
Interior Photos: Koji Hirano/Shutterstock Images, 1; BarryTuck/Shutterstock Images, 4–5; Shutterstock Images, 5; iStockphoto, 6–7, 7, 8; Alix Kreil/Shutterstock Images, 9; Sakdinon Kadchiangsaen/Shutterstock Images, 10; Numpon Jumroonsiri/Shutterstock Images, 11; Alison Hancock/Shutterstock Images, 12; wastesoul/iStockphoto, 13; Everett Historical/Shutterstock Images, 14; muratart/Shutterstock Images, 15; georgeclerk/iStockphoto, 16; jcarillet/iStockphoto, 17; Styve Reineck/Shutterstock Images, 18; AlessandroZocc/Shutterstock Images, 19; Sumiko Photo/Shutterstock Images, 21

Editor: Emily Temple
Series Designer: Madeline Berger
Art Direction: Dorothy Toth

Publisher's Cataloging-in-Publication Data
Names: Rivera, Andrea, author.
Title: Rocks / by Andrea Rivera.
Description: Minneapolis, MN : Abdo Zoom, 2018. | Series: Rocks and minerals |
    Includes bibliographical references and index.
Identifiers: LCCN 2017930290 | ISBN 9781532120473 (lib. bdg.) |
    ISBN 9781614797586 (ebook) | ISBN 9781614798149 (Read-to-me ebook)
Subjects: LCSH: Rocks--Juvenile literature. | Mineralogy--Juvenile literature.
Classification: DDC 552--dc23
LC record available at http://lccn.loc.gov/2017930290

Table of Contents

Science 4

Technology. 8

Engineering 10

Art 14

Math 16

Key Stats. 20

Glossary 22

Booklinks 23

Index 24

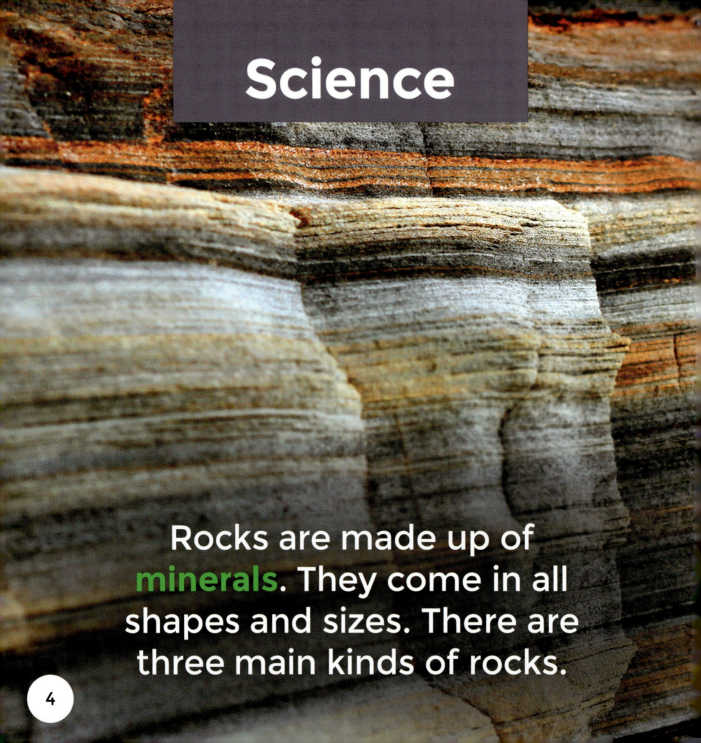

Science

Rocks are made up of **minerals**. They come in all shapes and sizes. There are three main kinds of rocks.

Igneous rocks form from hardened **magma**.

Sedimentary rock forms when many bits of sediment are pushed together.

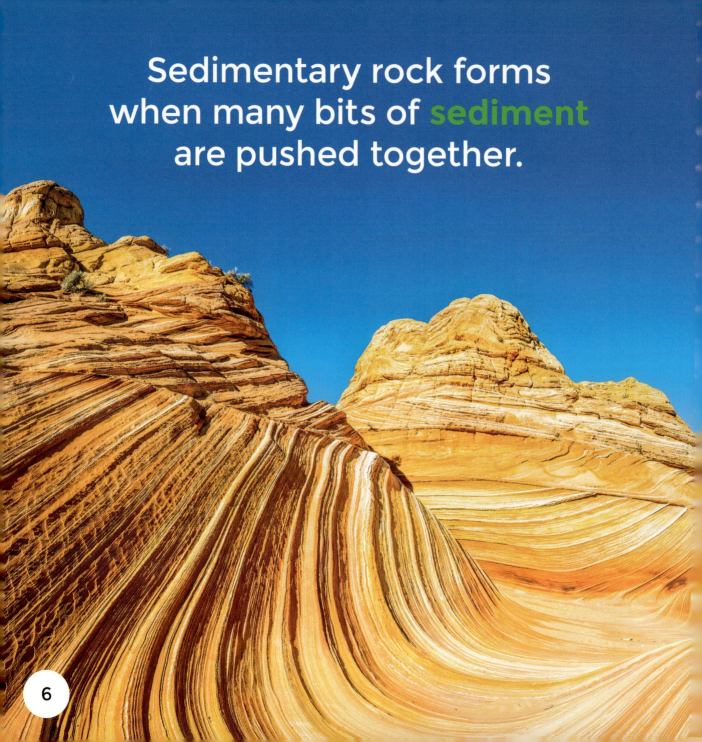

Metamorphic rocks form when heat or **pressure** is put on a different type of rock.

Technology

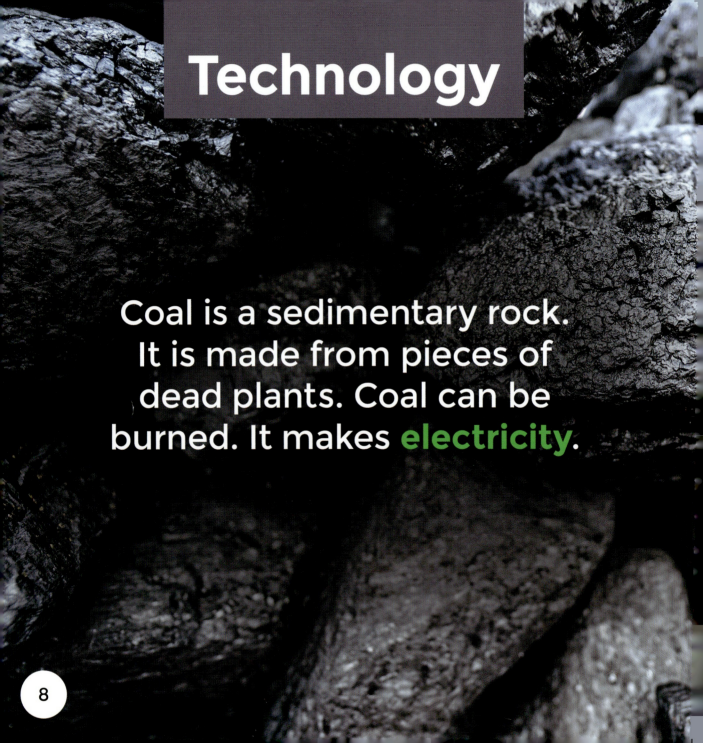

Coal is a sedimentary rock. It is made from pieces of dead plants. Coal can be burned. It makes **electricity**.

Electricity powers things like machines and lights.

Engineering

Rocks can be used to make many things. Limestone is a rock.

It is crushed and heated.
This makes cement.

Cement is mixed with water, sand, and bits of rock. This makes concrete.

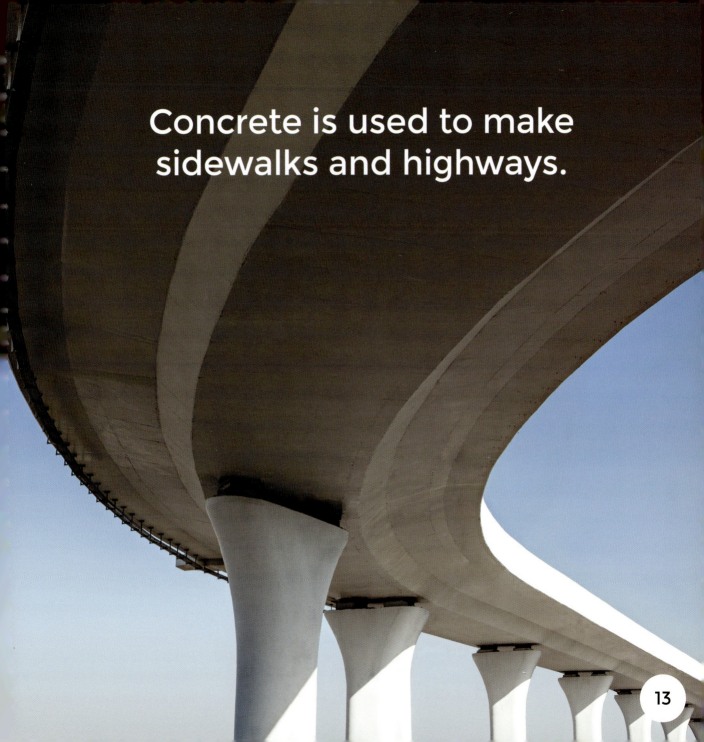

Concrete is used to make sidewalks and highways.

Art

Michelangelo was a famous artist.

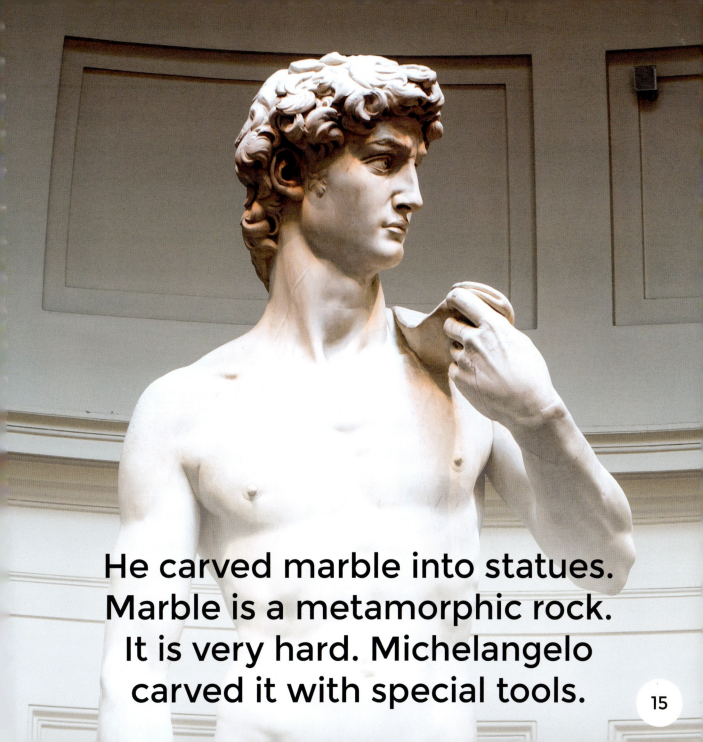

He carved marble into statues. Marble is a metamorphic rock. It is very hard. Michelangelo carved it with special tools.

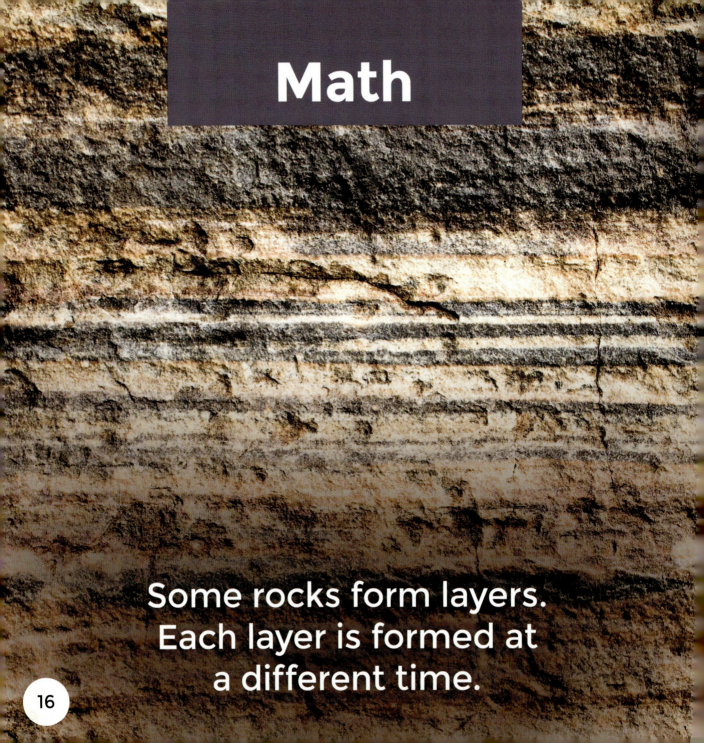

Math

Some rocks form layers. Each layer is formed at a different time.

Deeper layers have older rocks.

The layers can hold **fossils**.
Fossils in deeper layers are older.

Scientists can learn what was alive at different times by the depth of fossils.

- The Grand Canyon is made from igneous rock. Pumice is also a type of igneous rock. It forms when a volcano erupts.

- Limestone is a sedimentary rock. So are shale and sandstone.

- Marble is a metamorphic rock. So are soapstone and slate.

- Chimpanzees use rocks as hammers. The hard rock can break open the shell of a nut.

Glossary

electricity – a form of energy that can be carried through wires.

fossil – remains or impressions of a plant or animal from long ago.

magma – very hot, liquid rock from deep inside the earth.

mineral – a substance that forms naturally under the ground.

pressure – pressing or pushing against something.

sediment – tiny pieces of solid material such as minerals or sand.

Booklinks

For more information on rocks, please visit abdobooklinks.com

Learn even more with the Abdo Zoom STEAM database. Check out abdozoom.com for more information.

Index

cement, 11, 12

concrete, 13

electricity, 8

fossils, 18, 19

igneous rock, 5

layers, 16

limestone, 10

magma, 5

marble, 15

metamorphic rock, 7

Michelangelo, 14

minerals, 4

sedimentary rock, 6, 8